WRITINGS FROM A CROWDED MIND

BOOK TOO

poems

GERMANUEL B. LEA, JR.

WRITINGS FROM A CROWDED MIND

BOOK TOO

This book is dedicated to the most wonderful, loving and kind woman, who knew me well. My wife, Rev. Dr. Laura B. Lea. For Forty-Two years we shared a life together. Our children never knew us to be anything, except together and happy. Besides being my wife and a virtuous woman, she was my lover and my friend.

She used to say, and I quote: "If I'm mad at you, I end up talking to you about you, because you are my best friend". I remember those conversations that kept us together for Forty-Two years, because it worked both ways. We did not invite outside factions in to tell us about one another.

Through our friendship, we found a way to solve all our issues, and we thanked God for his presence in our relationship. I will miss you, my wife, my woman, my lover, and my friend.

CONTENTS

THE ACTS OF A DARK HEART

The Dark Heart is a place of emptiness. It is controlled by a twisted mind focused on itself as the controlling factor for all things. It embraces selfishness before and in the position of power. Its only friends or allies are those who embrace its goals of placing others in a state of obedience and servitude thru lies and innuendos told as trues. Sworn to often enough to create doubt of the truth you see and know. It is steeped and steamed in Hatred simply for the cause of success in its mission.

The Dark Heart lives in the fear of Love and Truth, so they speak sternly with conviction and the attitude of truth while lying and robbing and devaluing life itself. The Dark Heart has no conscience, only fear that it may be found out before it rises to control. Hence, as it moves forward, it creates roadblocks to maintain its position as the answer, all done while crippling the truth and eroding its foundation. Roadblocks that undermine what they once swore to protect but are now for empowerment.

Proudly, they ask for your support to rob you of stability. To help enrich them while poverty moves upward for you under their control. To help build a nation on the basis of color, ethnicity, ruling greed, and increasing poverty.

SCARECROW

It was a time of change for the nation. The populace had listened to the voices and ideologies of the would-be leaders, one stood above the rest. They chose that voice, that fresh face, with the sincere smile of confidence to step forward. To become their new leader. But the ScareCrow of Hypocrisy awaited.

He and his minions chose the path of Imperious resistance. Granting pretentious recognition and crippling progress, their stance veiled under the guise of Political Differences. While the Nation suffered, critical needs went unmet, and Democracy developed an Asthmatic Condition. Self-righteousness would be upheld. While the cry for change was muzzled as if it were a vicious dog.

Once, the ScareCrow of Hypocrisy stood proudly in his efforts to defend his version of democracy. Magnificently radiant in his stoic defense against political change. Today, he's quiet, subdued and apprehensive of a movement gone mad. Regret fills his eyes and heart as he watches in silent remorse the demise and decay of democracy. Shaken to the core of his being by the movement towards an Authoritarian Dictatorship.

Truth has been abandoned, and twisted lies have become foundational truths. Fear has become the preventer of Honesty, the Crippler of Negotiations and the Silencer of Wisdom. Democracy now has COPD. Now the Fascists, the Racists, the Separatists, and the Arrogantly Self-Centered seek power for themselves and a would-be dictator. A person seeking power, fame, and control for the sake of ego and self-glory.

Now the ScareCrow speaks quietly and sits confused in the Arena of Calamities once known as Government.

THEY RAPED THE WHITE HOUSE?

On a chilled day in January, a call went out to defend a lie. A call to bring about the change of a Validated, Sanctioned, and Recognized decision—and it was heard. A crowd of people answered the call. Yielding themselves to the rallying of a man who would not accept defeat. A man whose victory existed only in his mind, and the mind of those that would follow him. And for that cause, they Raped the White House.

The incited crowd rallied to the White House, gathering energy and anger from the call. As they reached her defending barricades and fences, they were in full riot mode. Screaming, Yelling, and Threatening her defenders, they moved forward. Forward on a mission of obedience to their caller. Rallying to a lost cause and Disrupting the Democratic process, for the sake of an attitude, while defending a lie.

Soon they assaulted her defenders. The defenders, now battered and bruised, retreated to defend her from behind her walls. When rage reached its climax, they began her rape in earnest.

They began scaling her walls as a rapist would remove clothing to obtain his objective. They broke out her windows, as a rapist would punch his victim in the face, for intimidation, to weaken her resistance. Moving forward, they tore the doors from their hinges, as a rapist would force open a victim's legs to gain entry. With her defenders in retreat seeking to save lives and crying for help, now she lay open to assault.

Her assailants now strode her halls, filled with the blossoming pride of their success. As a rapist glorying over his victim, who has no will left to fight, they abused her again and again while answering the call. The call of one seeking empowerment of himself above Democracy. For this cause, they Raped the White House.

REMEMBERING EMMETT

The world remembers Emmett Till, a young man with laughing eyes, Rubenesque cheeks and a welcoming smile. To himself, a young man coming of age. To his mom he was her baby boy, her child, who she watched over like a lioness protecting her cub. To himself, he was a young man in the know, he was not momma's baby boy. He was visiting Mississippi, all wired up with a young man's persona of coolness. Little did he know or understand, it was the beginning of his end. He paid homage to a Southern Belle, a woman of great beauty and a cold heart, when it came to Emmett.

Was it a wolf whistle? I don't know. Was it a lingering and a youthful flirtatious smile as he paid for his purchase? I don't know. What was important, and that he didn't understand, his man-child compliment was insulting to the Southern Belle. Why? Because he was a Black Man-Child, whose mere presence was an annoyance to her. His cousins cringed in fear for him, as he smiled at his manly deed. He did not understand that in Chicago it was charming, and may have brought a smile, in Mississippi, it was deemed a crime, because he was a young Black Man-Child. He didn't know that Death was on the horizon.

Sleeping soundly from his day's journey, he lay resting with the other children. His kinsmen stood and sat nearby, waiting for the worst, praying for the best and for his safety. They were people who lived in fear of the pagan self-righteousness that would take his life.

Emboldened by alcohol they came. Armed with the shield of Racist Self-Righteousness, they put forth their demands for his presence before them. Fear kept his kinsmen in check, there was only a token of resistance. Instead, there was begging and pleading for understanding and mercy for a child who didn't know he had committed a crime. For he possessed no knowledge of the racist guidelines of behavior, he was only complimenting beauty. They took him, enraged with self-serving pride and guarded by injustice.

Three men took a child to their place of reckoning, a place where suffering would make death a sweet relief. Where no doubt, he pleaded and cried for mercy. Perhaps even called for his mother, but the torture didn't cease until the silence of death. Then three grown men admired and bragged amongst themselves and later to others, about their great accomplishment: torturing a child to death. Self-righteous glory knows no boundaries of depravity. Emmett's mutilated body told this truth.

A body, that despite outcry, was placed in an open casket for the world to see and to testify to culturally supported brutality. This was done in a nation known for Democracy, Equality, and Justice for all. But for some, Inequality and Injustice are the pillars of democracy.

If, like me, you remember Emmett. If, like me, you remember the situation. If, like me, you remember the verdict and the celebration of injustice. Then you understand why Lady Justice is Blindfolded, Equality is a mere Philosophy, and Democracy a fading Fantasy.

I Remember Emmett.

DEATH OF AN INNOCENT

For Tyre, it was the end of a wonderful night. A night spent with friends laughing, talking, and even singing the songs they enjoyed. Now he was headed home with fond memories of a good time. For him home was in the near distance, a picture set in the framework of his mind. A distance he would not reach and a view he would not see again. He heard the sounds of the sirens and saw the flashing lights. Unknowingly, he obediently pulled over unto death.

Greeted with a vicious verbal onslaught, given no reason for his stop, joy turns to fear. He is roughly handled and placed in handcuffs and surrounded by five officers. He knew abuse was inevitable, but he did not know that death was imminent, for his arrestors were Black MEN, like himself.

The fear of inflicted pain becomes a reality. The verbal barrage of disrespect is lost to the pain of physical abuse. As he groans and cries out after each blow or kick. Perhaps a small corner of his mind tries to reason, Why? But no answers are found within himself. Only the abusers know their cause and objective for their actions. He only knows the pain of their assault, for they have become drunk on the power of abuse.

What did they seek?

Tyre became a martyr representing injustice at its apex.

They became infamous murderers and disgraced officers.

Were they sending a message to criminals?

Tyre was an innocent man going home.

They have become criminals.

For what reason was this done? How did it go all wrong? What was the trigger for this action? Why him?

Perhaps, from the grave, Tyre's one question:

WHY ME?

THE NO-KNOCK WARRANT

The No-Knock Warrant is a tool for the Police, often misused, and brings about grief, sorrow, and shame. A paper that is supposed to be Verified, then Certified, before being Activated. Its Activation represents undeniable certainty that a criminal is in residence. But we know this has not been so.

Addresses prove to be wrong, or the criminals have moved on, leaving INNOCENT people caught in the midst of a legal storm. A storm that produces Unlawful Entry and as well as Wrongful Death, simply because protocol was not followed.

Apologies have been made, justifications attempted, but how can you validate or justify the loss of life, or the embarrassment to both Police and victim? Words cannot cover up wrongful death or home invasion nor alleviate damage done.

The wrongful death of a young woman, asleep in her bed. Her defender charged and arrested because the intruders were Policemen not burglars. A No-Knock Warrant: Activated Validated?Truthful?□Enforced, to be the home of a criminal.

A No-Knock Warrant: Activated□Validated?□ Truthful?□Enforced, A mistake that traumatizes a mother and her children. An innocent child, scared for his life as he stands before the Policeman asks, in wide-eyed fear, Are you going to kill me?

A No-Knock Warrant: Activated□Validated?□ Truthful?□Enforced, A mistake, as a tired woman enters her home, and begins to relax in her shower. Suddenly she hears her door shatter and the cries of, Police! Police! Removed from her shower, Naked and Wet she CRIES, You have the WRONG HOUSE! And so, it was.

For the MISTAKES made, there will be insincere apologies and Contrived excuses. There will be monetary settlements awarded which create instant millionaires. But money will not replace the MOTHER who died. Nor will it detraumatize a young child, who now lives in fear of the Police. Nor will it remove the stigma of embarrassment while standing NAKED before the Police.

THE RUNNING MAN

He was a Running Man who loved to view the city streets or the countryside, not from the seat of his car, but from the drive of his legs. For him exhaustion equaled exhilaration, enjoying the sights and sounds of nature, and the lay of the land afoot.

He ran to see what was around the next corner or just over the hill or perhaps what was at the end of the lane. He ran waving to people, greeting others with an outstretched hand and a warm smile. He ran unaware or perhaps just assuming no one would harm him. However, he was wrong. Just around the corner lay Anger, Hatred and Death.

Men who found his mere presence offensive, to their sense of values. After all, he was a Black Man in a White neighborhood. A neighborhood where he wasn't wanted, nor would he be tolerated to simply pass through without confrontation.

They shouted at him, rather than greeted him. They cursed him, rather than welcomed him. They made an attempt to arrest him simply because he was there and a Black Man. He ran, they trailed him in a truck. He was now on the run. Not for the sake of the joy of running, but for the preservation of his life. For he was now a hunted man.

Why? Because self-righteous Hatred has no boundaries it merely dictates action be taken. Hence an innocent man suffers the injustices of racism. Being found guilty of being a Black Man in their space.

His run is now ending, not with the joy and exhilaration of life itself, but with the thud of Death. From this, he cannot rest and run again.

SHE WAS NAKED

It was the end of a tedious workday, and she was looking forward to the peace and quiet of home. Where there would be silence and perhaps soothing music at the end of day, but it was not to be so. In the midst of her soothing and massaging shower, covered in a warm tension relieving lather. She was disturbed as she was naked.

Suddenly there was the explosion of the splintering door. Followed by scampering footsteps and loud voices shouting, Police! Police! In a terrified voice she screams, You have the WRONG HOUSE! You have the WRONG HOUSE!

They find her and remove her from the shower, not allowing her to cover herself. Standing stark naked before twelve Police officers, for what seemed to be an eternity. Covered only by the thin sheen of drying moisture from the shower, folded arms, and cascading tears down her cheeks, she was naked.

With a No-Knock Warrant, they had entered her home. A warrant whose issuance validates the presence of a criminal on the premises, but it was not so. Before them in her home, she stood an innocent, frightened and naked woman, frantically trying to cover herself with hands and arms. The warrant had not been factualized before issuance, now they were in the center of a strained and embarrassing situation, and she was NAKED. Covered only by the invisible cloak of shame, she kept repeating, *You have the WRONG HOUSE!*

After a thorough search, they found nothing linking her to a criminal life. Then she was allowed to cover herself. Empty apologies came forth, as they realized the error they had made. Later would come a generous financial settlement to compensate for their bold ineptness. Will cash cover the shame, the embarrassment, or the impacted memory of being NAKED before them?

CRYING IN THE SILENCE

Can you hear the crying in the silence? The cries of those who died for reasons unknown to them. The cries of those who died because they were there that particular day. A day chosen by the killer to be his day of reckoning upon a society that had lost awareness of him. A society to which he had become invisible, but now they would hear and see him through the deaths of innocents.

Can you hear the children of Sandy Hook, Uvalde, and other schools, despondent pleas not to die? Can you hear their whimpers of despair falling on deaf ears and empty hearts? Can you still hear the screaming and see the shock on faces shopping in a mall, which has become a killing field. Can you hear the screaming confusion of an audience, turned into a frightened mob as they realize they are now targets of anger?

I can hear the Crying In The Silence, I can feel the pain of the lost who died for another person's dysfunctional rage. My emotions are aflame, for I can hear the sobbing and cries of affected families, asking Why. But the loudest and most disturbing sound I hear is the word NO to changing GUN LAWS.

New laws that would not cripple the right to bear arms but enhance the prevention of the misguided to obtain arms. Laws that would make the Black Market, change its approach, slow it down, for we know it can not be stopped. But can we bring about a continued limp, that could save lives, children's lives?

From somewhere in the crowd, let the Cry for Life become overwhelming. Even more so than the Cry to hold destructive life taking unconscious metal, wood, and plastic. Which, without restrictions, get to be directed to hallucinating, self-absorbed malcontents, whose desire has become to take lives.

Not just any lives, but the lives of those who know nothing of their plight or perceived troubles, the Innocent. School Children, Welcoming Worshipers, Unexpecting Shoppers, and Entertainment Attendees, none of whom are aware of their crimes or guilt. They have no knowledge of their killer's cause, whether it be Hatred, Discontentment, or Emotional Distress that's self-imposed. But the answer to their problem is Death to the Innocent and the Unaware.

The route to Gun Ownership needs to be altered for the sake of society. So that there may be far less funerals of the innocent. So that it is more difficult for the troubled to obtain guns. So that the Black Market is leery and slow to operate. We may never stop the Crying but we can act to move the Crying farther apart.

FOR THE GOOD OF THE PARTY
AND THE DEMISE OF THE DEMOCRACY

America is dying for the Party. A now misguided Party that is misrepresenting the truth and pounding lies, as truth, for the sake of Party Unity. In the path of this forged Unity is Democracy. As the Party unites in its division, Democracy faces the struggles of its fractures.

Moral men and women are seemingly prisoners of fear and retaliation from their brethren in government. The reigning puppets of a would-be Dictator working to dismantle Democracy. Working with deceiving smiles and twisted ideology that looks pleasant but cripples functioning government. As they support the Rioters, Assaulters, and Separatists they fled from during the misguided confrontation and were hidden by devoted Security Officers. As soldiers, they would be charged with Cowardice in the face of the enemy. For decisions made, which changed the course of truthfulness, for the situation they were in, they could be charged with collusion.

Their decision empowered the Racists, Separatists, Liars, the Greedy, and the Self-Righteous desiring to rule. They have become the face of the enemy seeking to Destroy Democracy. Some are afraid to walk uprightly as before, negotiating in good Faith for the sake of the country. Sitting quietly in denial of wrongs being pushed forward as an alternative saving Democracy. Remaining silent to save a job already lost. A job dying a slow Death from the Shame and Embarrassment of Inaction to save Democracy from the Predators.

The moral majority sits in silence and fear of antagonizing the loud and often violent minority. A crowd set into motion by lies and covered by the political movement of the power-hungry. The willingly disoriented puppets who hear their truth, move forward for the commander, disrupting the nation. Democracy is fast becoming the hostage to an Authoritarian Movement hidden in a blanket called Democratic Change due to Political Differences.

Because now truth is fragmented into fashionable lies to meet an extreme purpose. Hence the truth, which you saw, becomes questionable, to the point of mental fatigue and disorientation as it is hammered with the Lie. As Afro-Americans and Hispanic Americans watch their votes become diluted and powerless in the adjusted system. Jewish Americans and Asian Americans watch for the restrictive laws in the midst of Hateful attacks upon their personage. As women lose the right to govern their bodies and Doctors could be jailed for giving needed treatments. Will women become citizens with no rights except to exist?

Will our society become a system of Taliban rules and laws under Communistic Law, disguised as an Alternative Democracy? Does Democracy now prepare for Burial in an unmarked grave after being Castrated of meaning and reformed to Death? While Moral Leaders say nothing, hiding in plain sight. Grumbling among themselves, making no statement, deserting Democracy with a powerful Inaction, as Taps is preparing to Sound over Democracy.

THE DEFENDERS & THE DESERTERS

They were the Defenders of the White House. Their duty is to protect Her and those who work within Her walls. In a strange turn of events, they had been called to service. They had faced a marauding mob on a mission of destruction to Democracy.

They had been forced to retreat to the legislative halls and move its attendants to safety. They all followed willingly, knowing the mob was a danger to all. For they were answering a call for personal empowerment above democracy.

The Defenders had laid their lives on the line not for pay or fame, but to answer the threat placed before them, a threat to the democratic process. Now in the Halls of Justice, they stood proudly, with scarred bodies and damaged psyches. Expecting a united conviction from those they saved, but they heard deserters. Those who expressed denial of the factual and actual incident.

Men and women who had followed them to safety in fear of their lives now told another story. They now supported the rioters, even creating a scenario in which the mob meant them no harm. Had they forgotten it was a riotous mob, not a tourist group? How could they forget the scars borne by the White House and those that stood before them? How could they overlook the broken windows, missing doors, and broken furniture? Somehow, all these facts evaporated in their new stance.

Now once proud and truthful men and women who defended Democracy had become pawns in a power play. A nation watched them embarrass themselves as they deserted the truth for a false sense of unity. If you listen closely and carefully you can hear the Death Bell ring: As truth lies on the floor from a fainting spell,

Decency stands in the corner astonished, and Democracy has developed a limp.

How will we respond to this situation? What will we support? Will we desert our intelligence and become blind followers nodding in agreement as decency and democracy fade? What will we empower? Will we be Defenders or Deserters?

WAS NIKITA RIGHT?

Nikita Khrushchev was a proud and boisterous Russian Premier. He told America and announced to the world his intentions: "We will bury you." My question to you is: Was Nikita Right?

Will Communism overtake Democracy and make the freedom of the people an illusion of existence? Where laws are written and controlled by the self-righteous, under the control of the greedy. While the moral majority refuses to step forward, because of their fear of the immoral and loud minority. Who announce their presence loudly and sometimes brutishly, as they support lies relentlessly.

In an open Democratic Society, all votes count. In a controlled democracy, only the votes for the ruling party counts. Somehow, others are found to be invalid for the good of the country or is it for the continued empowerment of the party?

In a Democratic Society, Lying and manipulating the truth are crimes against the nation and its people. In a Controlled Democracy, Lying and Manipulating the truth are but basic tools for empowerment to play on the minds of the people. We are told not to trust our eyes, and to close our minds to the Truth. We are asked to follow misleading rhetoric with supportive joy and dulled minds.

Minds that accept being misled for the sake of political unity. Misled for the empowerment of the self-serving. We are asked to submit a Blind Eye to open collusion that will open the doors to Dictatorship, which we believed would never touch our shores.

We the people, elected officials to protect our Democracy, our Freedoms, and our rights to flourish as a free people. Instead, a

Controlled Democracy is under Construction. A Democracy where the rich are protected and the marginal, the poor, and the middle class are taxed to death, for the sake of "economic growth for all" that becomes impossible. A controlled Democracy is secretly and openly a consent to a Living Dictatorship.

Is this happening? Are we rushing into a Dictatorship of our own accord, of our own free will, while waving the banners of political differences, are we Dialing up a Dictatorship, where only the Politicians win and their supporters and followers are empowered?

Let us think for a moment, "Was Nikita Right?" Will political differences do what the threat of nuclear war could not? Can his victory be brought about because of our differences and the silence of those, in the majority, who sit quietly while the enemy digs in? Are we a nation burying ourselves in a Communist-style Government, for the sake of Self-empowerment, Racism, Intolerance, and United Self-Righteousness.

"Was Nikita Right"? Will we the voters realize we may be endorsing Democracy's end? Are we willing to suffer the long-term consequences of our decision? Is democracy becoming a restrained and altered thought, rather than a system of Government?

"Was Nikita Khrushchev Right?"

THE BARBARIANS ARE AT THE GATES

This land called the United States of America, a country born out of frustration and a desire for freedom was once ruled from afar, and unfairly taxed and restricted. Yet, the people came together, to defeat an organized army and its confederates and established Democracy. Democracy: A system of government that tries to rightfully represent its people and itself. But now, the Barbarians are at the Gates.

America has stumbled, she has been quite sickly, but never failed to rise above the claws of destruction: Racism, Slavery, Civil War, and Self-Righteous Hatred. They all have been stalled and placed on their knees before Democracy. But now some have arisen, once more, in this monumental moment of change, with great impact and disruption. For now, the Barbarians are at the Gates.

They are not outside the Gates seeking to get in, but inside the Gates looking to Cripple Democracy. Hoping to open the Gates to the Probability of a Dictatorship draped in racism, clothed in Authoritarianism, garnished in Communistic Law, flavored with Taliban rules and regulations, sauteed with inflamed hatred. A place in which Lies, Greed, and monetary manipulation control government. Watch Intently, Listen Cautiously, as you are misdirected by crafted lies to create optimism about the loss of Democracy, the Barbarians are at the Gates.

They come to the Gates with the Sledgehammer of Self-Righteousness. Their way is the only way. Driving home the Wedge of Lies to open a Gap. Inserting the Pry Bar of Deceit to increase tension. The Hinges of Democracy weaken, and the Gates' Alignment is strained from the continuous onslaught. Yet, Democracy stands, as she is hammered, pried, and wedged again and again. She's gauged, dented, and scarred but not broken down. The Barbarians are assaulting the Gates.

Now the question is, Will there be an uprising large enough to overcome the mounting intimidation? To halt the continuous rape of the truth and the desertion of reality to altered facts of empowerment. Will there be a rallying cry for Democracy? Will a silent majority arise in a convicting stance for reality and truth? It must be soon, for the Barbarians Are At The Gates.

THE ANTAGONIST

It was a day of mourning for a fallen hero. A man of the people, a man who had pursued justice for all. A man who had been abused, battered, and jailed by the hands of bigotry and injustice. Suffering at the hands of a contrived legal system for the sake of its self-maintenance. A man who fought for equality while standing before the army of inequality.

A man who stood for non-violence in the midst of violence against him. A man whose words stirred both the path to action and inaction. His words often fell on deaf ears and closed minds that defended the wall of injustice that confronted him.

On this day of mourning there would be speeches made and tears shed. There would be a feeling of loss because his actions and his cries for equality have been stilled. His non presence would be missed by both friend and foe. Some would cry for the hero gone to rest, a man who in the face of villainy, did not wince, nor soften his stance of freedom and equality for all.

People spoke from their hearts, their words seasoned with Love, Respect, and Pride, yet with a sense of uncertainty. For the questions now become, "Who will pick up his baton? Who will voice the rallying cry against inequality and injustice? Who will issue the change to the Racist, the Separatist and the simply hateful? Who would now become the Voice of Reason?"

The die has been cast, the mantle awaits, as the baton lies in the field of play, awaiting a new and fearless anchorman to restart the seemingly endless race for Justice, Respect, and Equality of all the American People. America needs a new Antagonist. A new James Lewis.

OF WHAT VALUE IS TRUTH?

In a nation where democracy is dying and has become as fragile as a thin crystal goblet. A nation becoming rooted in devaluing parts of humanity for the sake of greed, ambition, and self-righteous pride. A nation in which racism is sought to be reintroduced to maintain power. As once proud men and women of integrity desert truthfulness to become slaves of propaganda.

Of What Value Is Truth?

When we are told to doubt the facts, we see and embrace the lies we are told, something is amiss. Will we be content to be misled by egomaniacal personalities, seeking to lead us to servitude and impoverishment as they seek to become our rulers, rather than our representatives.

Of What Value Is Truth?

When the ScareCrow of hypocrisy can command the desertion of truth for devotion to a known lie. A lie based on a truth that has been seen nationwide, with unedited clarity. A lie told with such force of unity, that questions and doubts do arise in the nation, and reality fades into the distance of the governing plain.

Of What Value Is Truth?

Now a nation must look into and upon itself. It must determine what its representatives will look like to the world. What will its identity be? Will its leaders be fabricators of the truth or speakers of the truth? Will their concerns be human dignity or self-empowerment unto dictatorship? Will they honor all humanity or play to the racial pride of noisy dissidents?

Of What Value Is Truth?

We are a Rainbow Nation with the truth being that every race has contributed to its greatness, growth, and development. But there are those who seek to augment the facts and omit the truths to ease a guilt which is troubling. We are asked to live a life of blindness amid created fears behind a wall of indifference to the truth. We are asked to demote segments of our society to abuse and exclusion.

Of What Value Is Truth?

There is a saying that becomes critical to our well-being as a nation in times like these: United We Stand, Divided We Fall. If we open our eyes to the truths and the facts before us, what can we see?

Will the facts become the altered truths of our reality? Will the truth be lost in the alteration of the facts, creating new reality? Will eyes go blind, ears deaf to the point of enslavement, to the loud and unworthy liars? Will we, for the sake of our attitudes and emotions, abandon the truth to reach selfish goals?

A nation is dividing under the weights of Lies, Fears, Racism, and Self-centeredness as the presiding factors. Truth was once a valued commodity under which we flourished politically. It was a required element to lead and known liars were shunned. Now as a nation, we must decide,

Of What Value Is Truth?

THE ODDS WERE FIVE TO ONE

For a gambler, these are tantalizing odds, money making odds, the underdog has a marginal chance. A chance for an upset that might shock the betting world. The true gambler smiles at the possibility of his gain and places a sizable wager. But there are times in life when 5 to 1 means there is no chance to change the outcome. The loss is guaranteed, and the victory is assured, the underdog will lose.

The odds gave Tyre Nichols no chance for survival and mercy and grace could not overcome the strength of brutality. Apprehended by those who were supposed to represent justice, he only received injustice. Men who took an oath to protect and serve lost their way to the arousing strength of brutality. Why we ask, for the ugliness is: was it a Black-on-Black crime or was it a Blue-on-Black crime?

What was the objective of the arrest? What was the crime committed? For what purpose was he Insulted then Assaulted, and then Abused unto Death. Seemingly the objective became lost in the brutality, making them assailants rather than arresting officers. Was it to be a demonstration of obedience to the unwritten code for the arrest of a Black Man? Abuse before arrest, and injustice after and during arrest.

Why? as they say, becomes the elephant in the room. For what reason raises both hands and For what reason looms over the situation like a dark cloud. The five can summon no rallying point for themselves. Neither from their peers nor the public. A public whose damaged psyche only sees a young victim dying needlessly, and the unleashed power of Police Brutality. The five now stand as towering symbols of injustice.

In death, Tyre speaks from the grave, magnifying injustice, calling for changes to an unjust system of policing. The mention of his name invokes calls for reforms and reorganization in the justice process. Reforms that would ensure that a better quality of men and women dawn the uniform of a Police officer.

FOR THE SAKE OF JUSTICE TO ALL

THE VERDICT

To their amazement and astonishment, surprisingly they had been found guilty. It was a sudden shock to the system of false reality. A system that lived and thrived on justice by injustice, unanimously supporting judicial racism. The verdict brought a shout of joy from a grieving father, who was living on the fringes of hope and prayer that true justice would prevail.

He knew the system, he understood the verdict of choice for White on Black crime, disregarding the facts, Innocent would be the verdict of choice. His reality was another pleading prayer unanswered. Yet we know that miracles do exist.

Three men, who expected to be absolved from any criminal action, now face incarceration. Men who wore their crime with pride and self-serving dignity were now in a state of disbelief. For the verdict represented injustice, to them. Because it was based on adherence to the facts, not the decision of closed minds and blinded eyes.

Twelve jurors could not see themselves as accessories before and after the facts, seeing, hearing, and knowing the truth. Morally aware that it was a crime of self-righteous justice against a Black Man, who committed no crime.

A man who would have greeted them with a smile, extended a hand and offered pleasant conversation. Yet, he only received cursing's and threats, so he began his last run. Not a run for joy nor for elation, but, for the sake of his life. A life he lost to the purveyors' self-righteous judgment.

But now he has won, his death has received justice, in a system that stood for injustice. A system that had deserted so many that had gone before him. A system that upheld the rights to bigotry and murder above justice, for the sake of racism. A system that seems to be saying enough is enough, that hate, and injustice are no longer our common ground for Justice.

THE VERDICT TOO

Humanity is awakening from its blind endorsement of self-righteous crimes. Slowly the idea of a perpetrator's innocence because of race is fading to guilty because of the crime committed. The acts of abuse for self-serving pride and hatred are being seen for what they are, crimes against humanity.

In times past, it was a God-given right to perform such crimes against Black Humanity. Hangings, Beatings, Burnings, and Mutilations were the entertainment for social gatherings. They were endorsed and approved and used to ensure the power of Racism. In these Pagan practices of intimidation there was no wrong seen.

The offenders committed their crime emboldened by the past, and believed it would protect them in the present, for it had been so. But times are changing, and people are removing the blinders of agreement to needless and criminal behavior. They are now judging by the Known truth in their Hearts and the facts that are placed before them. Innocence is no longer determined by race and agreed upon lies, that are told in the boldness of truth. Guilty was the verdict, shock was the look upon their faces. Desertion was the feeling in their hearts, and amazement was the prevailing thought in the courtroom, thanks to a jury of their peers, who saw the horror of the crime. The uncalled-for and unneeded violence, for the sake of infamous glory and the expectations of being innocent. For after all, Ahmaud was only a Black man, an uninvited and unwanted Black man, jogging in their neighborhood.

The jury saw no glory nor anything honorable in this crime against an innocent jogger, who happened to be a Black Man.

Neither did they see a great service on behalf of the community. They saw only a needless murder defended by a contrived story, which the facts contested. Yet, they believed and expected that they would be found innocent, because of the past.

BLACK LIVES MATTER

Black Lives Matter, what is it? Is it a slogan for a people who are assaulted first, then arrested? Is it cry from the murdered victims, who were shot first then told to halt by a Policeman? Is it the teary voice of a young Black Man, who feels he was molested, rather than frisked? Is it a plea to the world to watch and take notice, as Black Men are abused, then accused of resisting arrest? Is it a crime to be Black?

For killing a Black Man, even if it was obviously murder, White men and Policemen have gone free. Free because according to the prevailing injustice system, it was not a crime, just an incident, and as a Black man, he was guilty of something.

Is Black Lives Matter a movement that started in peace, then highjacked by violent dissidents, who have disrupted its plea and reconfigured its identity through violence, robbery and destruction? Thereby masking its calling for justice and making it a pronounced criminal movement, creating a movement in turmoil searching for an identity.

Forgotten is the call for justice, forgotten is the plea for simple dignity, and unheard is the cry for equality. Remembered is the unrest and the violence incited by extremists. In a society adrift in hatred and moved more by violence than a prayer plea, what can be done? For hatred has castrated the movement toward equality to a mere crippled thought.

For Black America watches as the Jim Crow era seeks a rebirth. A system of racial indignities justified by self-righteousness and enforced by endless and senseless brutality. Because of the cancer called Racism; Black people are beaten, raped, shot, hanged, castrated, and murdered for the crime of existing.

Our Nation is a coalition of Identities, all of which have contributed to its national greatness and world appeal as a place to call home. Black Lives Matter is a movement in which all of America can participate. It is a movement in which Black Americans, White Americans, Indian Americans, Italian Americans, Jewish Americans, Mexican Americans, Asian Americans and Russian Americans and so forth can join in the cry for justice and equality for all. A union that brings to the forefront that every life matters.

ON THE HORIZON

A dreamer's eyes are always on the horizon, focused on what lies beyond that boundary. For the horizon is reachable, but when you get there its in front of you. The horizon is always a journey away from where you are.

In this world, the things we have created rested in the horizon of someone's mind. Who began a journey of mental and physical fabrications to create a solution to reach their horizon. At its completion, a new realization sets in, someone sees a new horizon before them. A new destination to trek toward.

Thinkers, Ponderers, and Dreamers know and understand the reality of the horizon. Their perception is true to its being. They know and understand the concept of its isness. The horizon cannot be captured but only reached for a moment, then it looms before you. It exists on a plain of unending vastness, there is always a horizon.

Physically and Mentally, you can travel the distance before you. A distance that can change your view, alter your perspective, and even give you that elusive answer you could not find. But remember and understand that at the end of your journey, The Horizon lays before you.

As we look forward, the next great creation or discovery is on the Horizon. That vast expanse that is continually growing and spreading before our eyes. We need a new mindset, an improved retrospect of reasoning, and a new creative attitude to reach the next connective Horizon.

LOVE IS BLIND

Love is Blind, it is an emotion that exists within us, and arises unexplainably. Love has no guidelines. To the disdain of some, it will cross ethnic and color lines. To some, its occurrence causes turmoil and personal stress to some. Love simply is its joy uniting and its presence comforting and elating. For some, this is a crime against humanity, and they loudly speak against it because the natural action breaks their imposed guidelines for love.

Today, as in times past, agitators are driven by personal judgements and hatred. Love doesn't listen to that. Hence the emotional unstable desire to be superior and controlling of love fail again and again. Why? Love does not understand laws, or the criminal actions done in its name, it exists simply for the joy of itself.

True Love does not arrest anyone nor sentence anyone to death nor disown or hate anyone. It simply brings happiness, peace and togetherness, unless disrupted by prejudices, which introduces sorrow for simply personal reasons. Loves only requirement is simply reciprocation of itself which causes it to expand and include others.

True Love does not function under a contrived sense of righteousness, with directions for disobedience and installed boundaries. Love wouldn't burn a church; how can you burn one in the name of Love? Love does not shoot someone in the back nor rape and murder or torture anyone to empower itself. Love doesn't celebrate itself in the joy of suffering deeds and seek approval for deeds of debasement in the name of Love.

These are deeds of selfishness, hatred, and twisted minds united in self-righteousness for their sake of empowerment. A place where we are told what to see, what, and who to accept in the name of Love. But True Love is Blind and Directionless.

JUST A SMILE

Young men are sometimes childish to the extreme: yet they consider it a show of masculine appreciation. I was in the crowd when she passed, strikingly beautiful, seemingly embarrassed by their show of admiration. She turned to view us. She was just looking at me, so I simply smiled. She returned my smile, and continued walking towards the horizon. Following her were our eyes, unheard words of admiration, a few whistles, and even a howl.

There are things that just cannot be explained, and only after the occurrence, do you understand. It was dinner time, my friends wanted liquid nourishment first—I wanted real food. Engrossed in the menu in the noisy and crowed dinning room, I heard a soft, yet strong voice say, May I join you? I looked up, it was her.

I don't know if it showed, but I felt like a kid at Christmas who had gotten exactly what he wanted. I tried to smile and hold my composure, without looking like a nervous Cheshire cat. Smiling, I said yes, and rose from my chair to seat her. We faced one another and introduced ourselves, then begin the introductory surface questions. We discovered some fascinating things and didn't understand how this was our first encounter. We lived five blocks from each other and worked in the same office building, although for different companies.

Along with our friends, we frequented the same restaurants, parks, bars, and theaters. How had we missed ever seeing one and another? Jacqueline and I melted into a romantic involvement, outside of the life we shared with our friends. Sometimes it had to be just us. Together we laughed and smiled at each other a lot.

Finally, I got enough nerve to propose, she said yes, we got married. I quietly said, Yahoo! and smiled.

Tonight, she is waiting for me at home. I stopped for wine and flowers for her and for our meal. It's an anniversary night, and we are dining wearing only our best, our SMILES.

HEARING AND LISTENING

In the journey of Life as men and women interact, Hearing and Listening become the foundation of missed and found relationships. Because early in their lives, women begin to hear and listen with their hearts and minds. Men are often in a state of delayed growth, where they only hear with a lustful mind. Often this is true for women, but men are the leaders in this part of the journey.

They see beauty before them, they are aroused, sometimes enchanted, but mostly they are lustful. The heart is not yet involved, unlike the women who stand before them, women, who have opened their hearts and minds to the process called love.

For some of the women, they see the change in the man as his heart opens. They watch as his heart becomes involved and his life centers around her, as much as her life already centers around him. Now they move forward, both in Love, Hearing, and Listening, with all aspects of their beings engaged in one another.

However, all too often, the women become victims of their emotions because of their hearts. While fully giving themselves to someone only seeking lustful control, not love. They become objects of use, rather than the focus of love. Yet for the sake of love they suffer, because they've given their heart, and the mind loses its sense of reasoning. While expecting a change that will not come, they exist in a loveless death, unto an empty life. That denies them the sense of love's full fulfillment.

Often, they awaken from this self-imposed hypnotic trance of love with a vengeance. Freeing themselves from themselves and their delusion, as well as the antagonists of their existence. With a renewed mind and a guarded heart, they set forth once again. Hearing and Listening for Love with a shield over their hearts.

LOVE IS BLIND TOO

Love is blind, it has no eyes, but it sees into the heart of the one you love. Love is an emotion that fits within itself. Love cannot be tied to social ideologies. Love will and does conflict with rules, regulations and guidelines, Love is understandable, but not explainable, or is it explainable, but not quite understandable?

Love does not abide by nationalities, customs, or rationality. Those who stress these as natural walls against Love, find them crossed and can be heard to say: "Love is strange". Love may arise at any time and at any place. Its only goal is for Love to be recognized, embraced, and enjoyed.

Insecurities will cause you to miss the isness of LOVE. That moment it just appears, and says, "I'm here, smile and embrace me". While you are thinking about it, trying to decide if its right for you, it may walk away. For love exists far beyond criteria not naturally within us.

You see, the essence of true love will make you embrace a stranger, ethnicity, and color of no importance. However, what is important is the relationship Love establishes between you. Love gives birth to family beyond bloodlines. It will cause you to give of yourself for the sake of others.

PASSION LIVED HERE

I'm standing in our bedroom, once we knew it as our Eden, our Paradise, and our place of Refuge from the world. Mostly, I recall that Passion Lived Here. If furniture could talk and walls were to speak, what would they reveal? If the mirrors were to present a replay of our Loving Engagements and the room echoed the sounds of our entwinements, our words of Passion? Would they know that love and lust existed here in equal expression?

My gaze languishes upon our now empty king-size bed, never to be filled again by us. Warming thoughts run through my mind and body, ecstatic memories of the Loving Lust that was ours, for Passion Lived Here.

Passion, that uniting element between a man and a woman in a unifying Love Life. Its foundation is spiritual, its expression is physical, its ending is climactic. Rooted in long deep lustful kisses, which ignite the urgency to come together. Desiring to process one another in the envelope called intimacy, with actions dictated by roaming hands and thirsty lips seeking fervent kisses.

Passion lived within us. The bed was our altar of dedication to ourselves. It was an emotional and physical sacrifice made to our union, our togetherness. A place where expressions are softly moaned in an urgency of need: Kiss me, hold me process my entire being with yours. Coming together as riders on a mission of physical necessity for one another. Striving for that deeply exhilarating and emotionally draining instance of fatigue known as the Climax.

That place where moans, gasping breaths, and now entwined and limp bodies seek the same resting space. The space where united bodies cling to one another in loving exhaustion. Because Passion has run its course. Now for a brief moment, time stands still. My fondest memory is that our revitalization arose from deep within us, from somewhere and somehow a deeper thirst arose, passion had reawakened on a higher, and yet gentler, level than before. Now with a softer and quieter urgency, we moved forward on a new journey, because Passion Lived Here.

It is quiet now and only the fading essence of your being lingers in the air. It is a fragrant memory to my mind and body. As I gaze upon the bed, Our Eden, Our Paradise, Our Altar. Memories rush in and with teary eyes I recall: Passion Lived Here.

FORTY-TWO (42)

Everyone has a favorite number, mine has become 42. It represents our 6 children, 4 boys and 2 girls, 42. Forty-Two, the number of years we had together.

For 42 years we had love and laughter within ourselves. For Forty-Two years we prayed for God's presence for others, to solve their problems and ours. For 42 years we wiped away tears, lifted praises, and as best we could, followed Gods spiritual directions.

Thank you that for 42 years you Loved me without interruption and unconditionally. Despite my faults, you gave me all of you. Your love, your trust, your devotion were mine and mine alone for 42 years.

Thank you, Laura, for 42 years. Forty-Two is my new favorite number.

GRANDPA'S REST

I watched Grandpa rise from the card table laughing heartily. There was a smile of happiness that came with the sight of accomplishment and success. My dad and he had just run a No Trump Boston, the supreme challenge for Bid Whist players. Now he was tired and needed a rest.

Grandpa's rest was strange to me, for how could someone rest so completely in the midst of the chaos of our family gatherings? But in each family home, there was a special chair for Grandpa. A recliner, from which he viewed not only the games on TV, but the gathered families.

Being inquisitive, I asked Grandpa, how can you rest so well, with all that's going on? The loud talk and laughter at the card table. The sounds of cheering or the groans of frustration, from those watching the games. The joyful sounds of giggling and loud conversations emanating from the kitchen and dining room. Grandpa, how do you rest?.

As he slipped into his recliner, "Lil man I'm surrounded by love. No matter whose home I'm in, love is my covering. For it is a gathering of loving, successful brothers, sisters, and cousins, in whom jealousy has no place. They are all at a degree of success for themselves, in which they live in pride, dignity, and respectfulness. Also, they are happy for each other. From the mechanic to the lawyer, from the doctor to the cook, love of family comes first. So, I can rest while in the center of my loving family, a family at Peace."

He slid into his recliner and pushed the button. It began its process. When it reached the desired position, he released the button. Then Grandpa stretched and shifted into his position of comfort and closed his eyes. A smile came across his face, a smile that you could tell came from deep within. A smile so glowing, that you knew there was a twinkle in his closed eyes, and Grandpa rested.

Life has been hard on me, even harsh to me, and I put everyone at fault: But me. It was my decisions that caused my problems. You see, I made bad choices, all by myself. I chose to continue when my friends chose to stop. I chose to drink, I chose to do drugs, I chose to live life as an unending party: they didn't. They walked away, leaving me to my foolish downfall, but my condition was their fault.

They walked away, I fell into depravity. Why? It was their fault, they should have been there to stop me. I became a functional alcoholic, never knowing when enough was enough. But I would always lie to myself and say: If they were here with me, I wouldn't be like this.

I left alcohol for drugs, but soon I united the two. My new existence became an unemployable alcoholic junky. Soon I was Stealing, Lying, and committing small crimes to support my bad habits. But it was not my fault. As it got worse, I knew the only thing left was prostitution, but I found myself refusing to sell myself.

Now I began to question myself for the first time. I accepted it was my decisions that brought me to this point. They decided to move on and prosper, now I knew that I should have agreed and followed. I now wanted a way out.

One night I found myself in front of a church, a church having a Revival. The joyous and resounding music pulled me inside. I was in need, soiled clothing, unbathed, and smelly. I entered expecting to be turned away, but I was not.

I do not remember the sermon, nor actually hearing the invitation to come forth, I only remember hearing the words, Come to Jesus. Everything was like an out of body experience that ended with me being in front of the church saying, "Thank you Jesus".

God placed me in a church that worked with the indigent. I was where I would be cleansed inside and out. God's changes seem to come quickly. I looked in the mirror one day and saw a peculiar person whose decisions were guided by prayer and spiritual awareness, not physical cravings.

I have become a completely different person, who is responsible for himself and thankful for the spiritual presence within me. I am now Clean, Employable, and at peace. I've become that good man I sought to be.

THE ACTS OF THE HEART

It is said that man's projection of a life well lived begins in his heart. Not the physical heart, but the deep-seated messaging center within himself. The unseen control point that decides what his truths will be. The place where ideologies of love and hate are fashioned and presented to the world—his public image.

On life's journey what is in the heart will be seen as who he or she is. It will determine whom they embrace or reject, and what their life's philosophy will be. Because Love is the first thing we learn and receive as babes and children. It is the first thing we must unlearn, far too often, in order to fit in. It does not matter what color, gender, or ethnicity, we embrace one another until we are invited into the world of differences.

We are given the words of change and encouraged to separate ourselves from those not like us. Things change and cause us to depart from our natural instinct to love everyone. The world introduces us to Hatred, Self-righteous Superiority, and Indifference to the lives of others. The invitational suggestions are: "They are not like us", "They are not as smart as us." And "They are not capable of _________."

We are asked to desert factions of humanity and embrace a selfish egotistical ideology. We are asked to join a faction that at any time can become our enemy, if we dare not to except their teachings. We are asked to quit sharing God's love and limit our love to those who look and think like us. We are asked to unite behind misguided ideas and lies, we are asked to become Hateful.

Love needs no training; it simply flows from one person to another freely. Love is an inborn condition; hate is a trained condition. Love makes you, or should we say, lets you embrace all humanity as your equal, and consider another as a human being worth of your kindness and love. Treating others with the Love and Respect, you want for yourself. God's Love gives the unexplainable knowledge that the only difference in man is what we make of them and how we embrace them.

Sensitivity and awareness to God's standards and His presence within you will keep you from engaging the fabricated data of superiority. It keeps you from emitting hatred and indifference from the core of your being. It will not allow you to commit, glorify, or justify crimes of hate, or use God as a crutch to commit any egotistical crimes. Acts of the Heart secure our place in eternity, as you live life, consider where your place will be.

ABOUT THE AUTHOR

Germanuel B. Lea Jr. is the author of *Writings From A Crowded Mind*. He was born on Aug. 29, 1947 in Columbus, Ohio to the parents of Ruth M. (Harris) Lea & Germanuel B. Lea, Sr., both deceased. Raised in East St. Louis, IL where he graduated from Lincoln Sr. High School in 1966. After being hired at Bethlehem Steel in July of 1969, he enlisted in the United States Army in January of 1970. Bethlehem granted Lea military leave during his enlistment period.

In November of 1973, Lea returned to work at Bethlehem Steel. Over a period of time, he attended the mill's Craft School and became an A-Rate Millwright. Bethlehem Steel was bought by International Steel Group (ISG), who then sold it to ArcelorMittal, from whom he retired, accredited with 43 years of continuous service. I am a father to six adult children and a grandfather to seventeen grandchildren.

He was happily married to the late Rev. Dr. Laura B. Lea for forty-three years. Together, they served at Life Temple Church of God In Christ under Elder Robert Flemming, in Michigan City, IN.

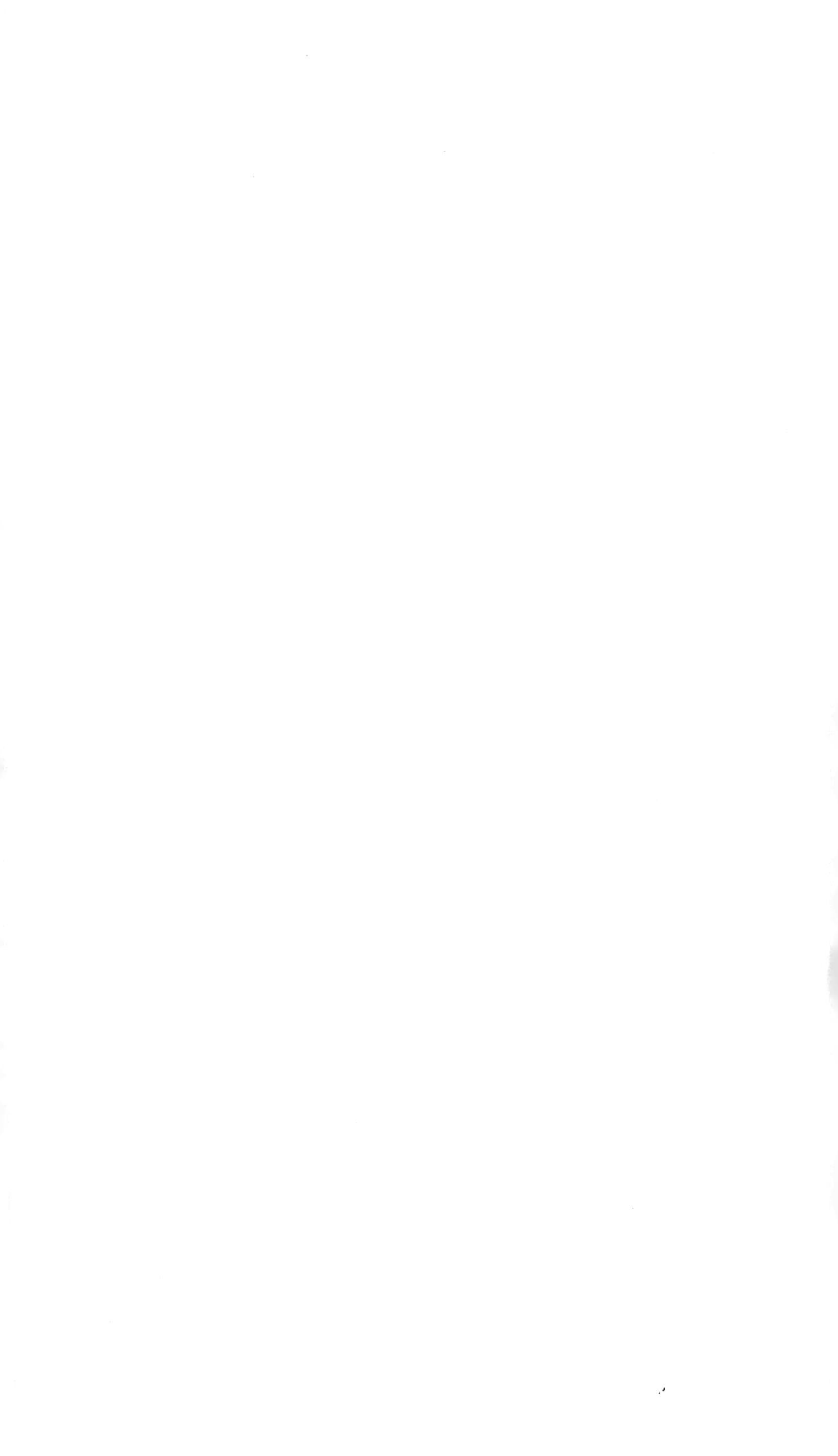

www.ingramcontent.com/pod-product-compliance
Lightning Source LLC
Chambersburg PA
CBHW040111150726
48005CB00013B/1657